Class :

Reptilia
(Reptiles)

Order :

Squamata
*(Snakes and
Lizards)*

Family :

Viperidae
(Snakes)

Genus :

Vipera
(Vipers)

Species :

Berus
(Adder)

to teachers and parents

This is a LADYBIRD LEADER book, one of a series specially produced to meet the very real need for carefully planned *first information books* that instantly attract enquiring minds and stimulate reluctant readers.

The subject matter and vocabulary have been selected with expert assistance, and the brief and simple text is printed in large, clear type.

Children's questions are anticipated and facts presented in a logical sequence. Where possible, the books show what happened in the past and what is relevant today.

Special artwork has been commissioned to set a standard rarely seen in books for this reading age and at this price.

Full colour illustrations are on all 48 pages to give maximum impact and provide the extra enrichment that is the aim of all Ladybird Leaders.

A Ladybird Leader

reptiles

written and illustrated by John Leigh-Pemberton

Ladybird Books Loughborough

Reptiles

Different kinds of
animals are grouped
in different 'classes'.

Mammals are grouped in their 'class'.

Birds, fishes and insects
are grouped in
their 'classes'.

Reptiles form
their own 'class'.

Agama Lizard
(Africa)

Leopard Snake
(S. Europe, W. Asia)

Reptiles have dry, scaly skin
without hair.

They breathe air,
and most of them
lay eggs.

Greek
Tortoise

They are
cold blooded.

So they must live in warm places
to survive.

Nile Crocodile *(Africa)*

5

American Crocodile

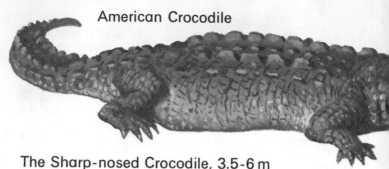

The Sharp-nosed Crocodile, 3.5-6 m
(12-20 ft), is found in Florida, Cuba
and south to Ecuador and Peru.

Crocodiles

There are sixteen kinds of crocodiles.

These reptiles live in lakes and rivers
in warm countries.

They are found in Africa, Asia,
America and Australia.

The Estuarine Crocodile, up to 6 m (20 ft) long,
lives in the mouths of rivers, from Sri Lanka,
through Indonesia, to N. Australia.

Broad-nosed Crocodile (W. Africa), 1.5 m (5 ft).
This small crocodile spends
much time in jungles.

There have been crocodiles on earth
for two hundred million years.

They are the largest reptiles.

Some can grow
to almost 9.1 m (30 ft).

They can live for fifty years.

This is the most savage of all crocodiles.
It has been seen far out at sea.

Hunting and feeding

Crocodiles are flesh eaters.
They eat fish, birds
and animals as big as horses.
They lie in the water
or on a sandbank,
and catch other animals
when they come to drink.

They grip their prey
in their powerful jaws.

Then they drag it under water
until it drowns.

Crocodiles also eat
any dead animals they find.

This sort of food is called *carrion.*

The Gharial (or Gavial), about 4.5 m (15 ft) long, is a relation of the crocodile. It lives in Indian rivers and eats only fish.

How they survive under water

Crocodiles live most of their lives in the water.

To do this they have some special muscles.

With these a crocodile can close its ears, nose and throat when under water.

Crocodile skin

The skin of all members
of the crocodile family
is covered with hard, bony plates.

This protects them from rocks
in swift-flowing rivers.

Crocodile leather is made
from the softer skin of the belly.

The Cayman is a kind
of South American alligator
from 1.8-3.6 m (6-12 ft) long.
It is protected all over with
hard scales.

Alligators

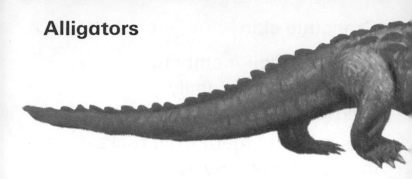

Alligators are related to crocodiles.

There is one kind of alligator in China and six kinds in America.

Alligators have rather blunt noses.

Their teeth are arranged differently from those of crocodiles.

Alligator

An alligator shows
only the teeth in his top jaw
when his mouth is closed.

A crocodile shows teeth
in both jaws.

These teeth are made for gripping
and tearing.

They are not used for chewing
or for cutting up food.

Crocodile

Alligators nesting

Alligators build large nests
made of mud and plants.

They are built on dry land.

The female alligator lays
about fifty hard-shelled eggs.

She covers these over
with leaves.

Baby alligators are 18 cm (7 ins)
long at birth. They feed themselves
on frogs and insects.

The heat of the sun
hatches out the eggs in ten weeks.

Just before they hatch
the young make a 'peeping' sound
from inside the egg.

The female opens up the nest
and the young crawl out.

Tortoises, Terrapins and Turtles

Leopard Tortoise
from Africa.

Tortoises, terrapins and turtles
belong to the same reptile group.

Tortoises live on land,
and turtles live mostly in the sea.

Terrapins are tortoises
which live both on land
and in rivers
and lakes.

Diamond-backed
Terrapin
from America.

All these reptiles are protected
by a hard shell.

This is in two pieces.

One, on top, is called the *carapace.*

The other, underneath,
is called the *plastron.*

Green Turtle
*(Mediterranean, Pacific
and Indian Oceans)*

17

Indian Starred Tortoise,
about 25 cm
(10 ins) long.

Food and breeding

The chief food of tortoises
is young plants.

They do not have teeth.

They munch their food
with a horny 'beak'.

All tortoises and turtles are probably deaf. Their ears are covered by a flap of skin.

Tortoises lay eggs
with a tough, leathery skin.

The female digs a hole
and lays her eggs in it.

Then she covers them with earth
and leaves them.

When they hatch, the young
have to fend for themselves.

Carolina Box Tortoise
from America.

How long do they live?

Tortoises can live
for more than a hundred years.

This is partly because
all their movements are so slow.

They are well protected
by their hard shells,
but birds and rats attack them.

Hermann's Tortoise from Mediterranean area.

When in danger the head and legs
can be drawn back
inside the shell.

In cold climates tortoises
hibernate (sleep) all winter.

In hot climates
they bury themselves in mud
during the dry season.

Giant tortoises

These live on the Galapagos Islands
and on an island
in the Indian Ocean
called Aldabra.

They are the biggest tortoises.

They often measure 1.2 m (3 ft 9 ins) long
and weigh more than 220 kg (480 lb).

They have become very rare.

Galapagos Tortoise

Terrapins

Terrapins are the smallest members of the tortoise family.

They have webbed feet, and live most of the time in water.

Many of them live in America.

Some, full grown, are less than 12.7 cm (5 ins) long.

'Roofed' Terrapin from India.

'Painted' Terrapin from America.

Leathery Turtle

Sea turtles

Sea turtles are found
in all warm oceans.

One kind, the Loggerhead, is
sometimes found in British waters.

The largest kind
is the Leathery Turtle,
which is about 1.8 m (6 ft) long,
and can weigh 590 kg (1300 lb).

The limbs of turtles are like paddles.
They eat mostly sea-weed.

Sea turtles—breeding

Sea turtles spend their whole lives
at sea,
but they have to come ashore
to lay their eggs.

They lay hundreds of eggs
in a pit on a sandy beach.

They dig this with their hind legs.

The young turtles hatch
in six weeks.

They find their own way to the sea.

Hawk-billed Turtle
laying eggs.

Snakes

There are more than
two thousand kinds of snakes.

Only about 250 of these
are poisonous to humans.

Snakes generally live
in warm countries,
but some kinds
can survive cold winters
because they hibernate.

The largest snake is the Anaconda
which lives in South America.

It can grow to 10.7 m (35 ft) long.

Most snakes
lay eggs which
have a leathery
shell.

Some have babies
which hatch out inside
the mother snake just
before they are born.

The word for this
is *viviparous*.

Anaconda

Snakes' food

Snakes kill and eat
other animals.

They eat their food
by swallowing it whole.

When they have eaten
they may go
for several months
before they eat again.

The American Scarlet
King Snake. It is
harmless to man but
eats other snakes.
It imitates the colouring
of the Coral Snake
which is very poisonous.

Copperhead Moccasin.
A very dangerous
snake from America.

Snakes' senses

Snakes have no eyelids
and no ear-drums,
but their tongues are
very sensitive.

They use them to test and taste
everything around them.

Their tongues flick in and out
all the time.

How do they move?

Humans have twelve pairs
of ribs.

Snakes have about two hundred.

They use the tips of their ribs
to help them move along.

They have no front or back legs.

Australian Diamond-backed Python,
4.8 m (15 ft 10 ins) long.

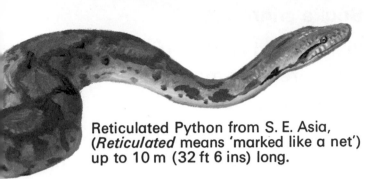

Reticulated Python from S. E. Asia,
(*Reticulated* means 'marked like a net')
up to 10 m (32 ft 6 ins) long.

Snakes' jaws

Snakes can open their jaws
very wide.

It is just as if they were
made of elastic.

A large python can swallow
a whole goat.

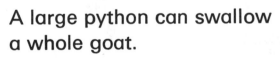

Snake charmers

In India and North Africa
there are showmen called
'snake-charmers'.
They keep snakes called cobras.
The cobras sway from side to side
as the man plays a pipe.

Cobras, like all snakes, are deaf.
They do not hear the music.
They sway to the pipe's movement.

Warning signals

Some poisonous snakes,
like cobras and rattlesnakes,
give warning before they attack.

The cobra spreads
a 'hood' at the
back of its head.

Cobra,
1.5 m (5 ft).

The American rattlesnake has
rings of hard skin at the end
of its tail.

It shakes these
to cause
the rattle.

Rattlesnake, 2.3 m
(7 ft 8 ins) long.

Grass Snake,
grows up to 1.2 m (4 ft)
and sometimes
much longer.

British snakes

There are three kinds of snakes in Britain (none in Ireland).

They eat frogs, lizards and mice.

The harmless grass snake lives in woods and marshes.

It is a very good swimmer.

It loves to bask in the sun.

The rare Smooth Snake,
grows up to 60 cm (2 ft) long.
It lives in a few places in S. England.

The adder is
the only poisonous British snake.

Like the smooth snake,
it produces live young.

The grass snake lays eggs.

They hatch in about eight weeks.

All British snakes hibernate.

Adder,
grows up to
60 cm (2 ft) long.

It can be told by the
zig-zag marking along
its back. It is the only
snake found in Scotland.

Emerald Tree Boa
from Australia,
up to 3.5 m
(11 ft 8 ins) long.
All the largest
snakes are
'constrictors'.

Constrictors

Anacondas, pythons and boas
kill their prey by squeezing it.

First they catch it with their teeth.

Then they coil their bodies round it
until it suffocates.

Snakes which do this
are called *constrictors.*

Snake skin

The skin of snakes
is not slimy.

It is dry and scaly.

Several times a year
the snake sheds its skin.

There is a new skin underneath.

This is called *sloughing.*
('slough' rhymes with 'puff')

Aesculapian Snake from S. Europe, 1.5 m (5 ft).
This shows the arrangement of scales.

Nose-horned Viper,
1.2 m (3 ft 11 ins) long.
One of the very poisonous
Puff Adders from Africa.

Poisonous snakes

Snakes like Cobras, Vipers
and Rattlesnakes kill their prey
by injecting poison into it.

They do this by biting it
with their special fangs.

The poison acts very quickly.

The poison is stored
in a gland in the head.

When the snake bites,
the poison flows down
a groove or tube in the fangs.

If the snake loses its fangs
it can grow new ones.

Adder's head
showing fangs.
The poison gland
is in the roof of
the mouth.

Anole Lizard,
20 cm
(8 ins) long.
It comes
from America.

Lizards

There are about three thousand
kinds of lizards.

They are found in all the warm
parts of the world.

Most of them have arms and legs.

There are five toes on each foot.

Only two kinds of lizards
have a poisonous bite.

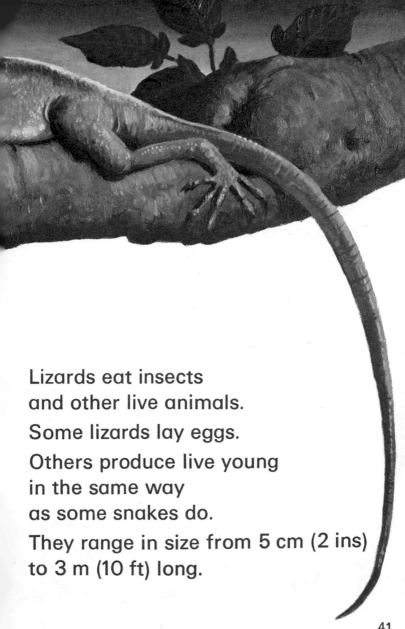

Lizards eat insects
and other live animals.

Some lizards lay eggs.

Others produce live young
in the same way
as some snakes do.

They range in size from 5 cm (2 ins)
to 3 m (10 ft) long.

Common or viviparous lizard,
9-18 cm (3½-7 ins) long.

British lizards

Three kinds of lizards
are found in Britain.

The Common lizard produces
from five to ten live young.

The Sand lizard is found
only in Southern England.

It lays about twelve eggs.

They hatch in about ten weeks.

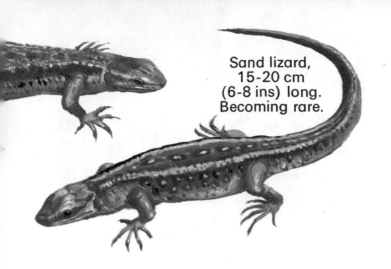

Sand lizard,
15-20 cm
(6-8 ins) long.
Becoming rare.

The slow-worm is not a worm
or a snake.

It is a lizard without legs.

Slow-worms lay about eight eggs
which hatch as soon as
they are laid.

Slow-worm,
28-50 cm
(11-20 ins) long.

Common Green
Iguana,
up to 1.5 m
(5 ft) long.

Iguanas

Iguanas are lizards
which mostly live
in the warm parts of America.

Some eat plants
instead of insects.

Most iguanas lay eggs
which are buried
until they hatch.

The Marine Iguana
is the only lizard
which lives partly in the sea.

It comes from
the Galapagos group of islands.

Seaweed is its chief food.

It swims and dives well.

It can walk on the sea-bed.

Marine Iguana,
up to 1.4 m
(4 ft 8 ins) long.
This one is from
Hood Island.
Large colonies
of them gather
on the rocks.

Giant lizards

The biggest lizards are
the Komodo 'Dragons'.
They live only on
a few small Javanese islands.
These powerful reptiles
can kill and eat
animals as big as deer.

Komodo Dragons belong
to the group of lizards
called *Monitors*.

Smaller Monitors are found
in Asia, Africa and Australia.

Komodo Dragon,
can be 2.7 m (9 ft)
long and weigh
130 kg (286 lb).
It lays up to 35 eggs.

Geckos

Geckos are the only lizards
which can make loud sounds.

They have pads on their toes
with which they can grip
any surface.

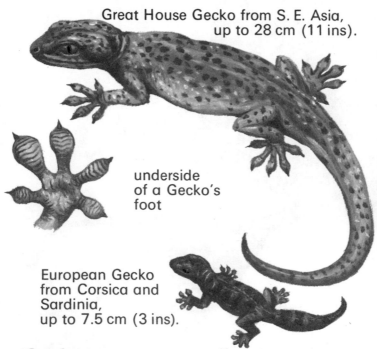

Great House Gecko from S. E. Asia,
up to 28 cm (11 ins).

underside
of a Gecko's
foot

European Gecko
from Corsica and
Sardinia,
up to 7.5 cm (3 ins).

Geckos can even walk
upside-down on a ceiling.

Skinks

Skinks form the largest group
of lizards.

Some have no legs.

Some have short legs and tails.

Others have very long tails.

Sand Skink from
the Sahara Desert,
20 cm (8 ins).

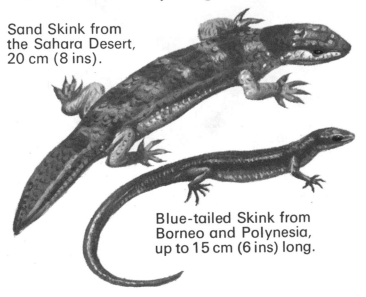

Blue-tailed Skink from
Borneo and Polynesia,
up to 15 cm (6 ins) long.

Like some other lizards,
a skink can lose its tail
and grow a new one.

Chameleons

usually about
30 cm (1 ft)
long

Chameleons can swivel
their eyes separately.

They can grip with their tails.

They can change colour
to match their surroundings.

They catch insects
with their long, sticky tongues.

The Tuatara —
a very ancient kind of reptile

In New Zealand there is
a rare reptile called the Tuatara.

It looks like a lizard.

But it is really a 'left-over'
from a group of reptiles
which lived millions of years ago.

Its eggs take a year to hatch.

Tuatara,
up to 62 cm
(2 ft 1in) long.
It lives in burrows
with sea birds.

INDEX